AN EDUCATION in schools and universities in Edinburgh and Glasgow, with degrees in Geography, Economic History and Education qualified Walter Stephen as an academic jack-of-all-trades with a lifelong devotion to environmental awareness and understanding, One of his achievements was the establishment and operation for 20 years of Castlehill Urban Studies Centre in Cannonball House in Edinburgh, the first successful Urban Studies Centre in Britain.

As former Chairman of the Sir Patrick Geddes Memorial Trust he has been responsible for several books around this famous polymath – *Think Global, Act Local, A Vigorous Institution, Learning from the Lasses, Exploration* and *Where was Patrick Geddes Born?*

In 2009, the Darwin year, he wrote *Charles Darwin – Some Scottish Connections* and *The Evolution of Evolution: Darwin, Enlightenment and Scotland.* He re-awakened interest in Frank Fraser Darling, the founder of ecology and forerunner of David Attenborough, by editing and having *A Herd of Red Deer* republished.

Willie Park Junior: The Man who took Golf to the World set the first golf professional to write a book about golf in a historical/ sociological context. This was followed up by the editing and republication of Willie Park's *The Game of Golf* and *The Art of Putting.*

In lighter vein *Walter's Wiggles: The Random Thoughts of Random Traveller* is a kind of a travel book in 15 chapters.

The Gypsy Empresses: A Study in Escapism looks at how the great ladies of five Empires found refuge fror ⸻ ⸻ ⸻ great affairs of state, especially on the Cc trees bloom'.

Ishbel Maria Marjoribanks
Marchioness of Aberdeen and Temair
Born 15th March 1857
Died 18th March 1939

the meddling marchioness in the north west

lady aberdeen in derry and donegal

walter stephen

Hills of Home
82 Pentland Terrace
EDINBURGH
EH10 6HF

hillsofhome@btinternet.com

First Published 2019

ISBN 978-0-9555190-5-5

Typeset by Colorprinz Ltd

Printed by Colorprinz Ltd

Contents
Illustrations – Colour Plates

Illustrations – Figures

Acknowledgements

It is entirely appropriate that I should begin these acknowledgements with three women. It was through Anne-Michelle Slater, Head of the Law School of Aberdeen University, from her chapter on The Noble Patroness Lady Aberdeen, that I first learned of the remarkable Ishbel. From the vast Geddes Archive in the University of Strathclyde Dr Anne Cameron was able to pluck evidence of Ishbel's work in Ireland and her association with the great planner, Patrick Geddes. Linda Ming, Heritage Collections Officer, Derry Central Library carefully navigated me through many distractions in the local newspapers of the 1890s.

The reporters and editors of the Derry Journal and Londonderry Sentinel of the 1890s deserve a mention for their very full, if occasionally balanced, coverage of things that interest me.

The human dimension was provided by my late mother-in-law, Daisy McBride and her neighbour, the last of the Derry shirtmakers, the late Arthur Hogg.

Out of an inchoate mass of material John Howie has produced a clean and handsome text. The unpublished PhD thesis of Frank Sweeney gives an excellent account of the condition of Donegal before the First World War, with no punches pulled.

The illustrations in the text referred to as Figs 2, 3, 4 and 5 and in the cover are reproduced by kind permission of the University of Strathclyde. Plates 3b and 4a and Fig 8 are reproduced by kind permission of Derry Central Library. The National Trust for Scotland have kindly provided Plate 1b. Plate 4b is reproduced by courtesy of CAIN . Fig 1 was provided by the Patrick Geddes Memorial Trust.
Every reasonable attempt has been made to secure permission for the reproduction of Plate 2a and Figs 6 and 7.

Other photographs are by the author.

The Meddling Marchioness in the North West
Lady Aberdeen in Donegal and Derry

THE PLOTS OF THE GREAT CRIME WRITERS of the 1930s, Agatha Christie, Dorothy L Sayers, Freeman Wills Crofts and many others, were so clever and complex that it was often felt necessary to have their characters listed and their relationships described, sometimes with a map or plan of the scene of the crime.

This story binds together at least three other stories, making it complex enough also to require a Dramatis Personae, the first on the list being **John Campbell Hamilton-Gordon (1847-1934)**, Earl of Aberdeen (created 1682), Earl of Haddo (1916), Viscount Formartine (1682), Viscount Gordon (1814), and Lord Haddo, Methlic, Tarves and Kellie (1682) in the counties of Aberdeen, Meath (Ireland) and Argyll. He was created Marquess of Aberdeen on 4 January 1916.

The Gordons were one of the greatest families or clans of the Highlands, with lands mainly in Aberdeenshire. *Glenlogie* is one of the great ballads of the North East, first published in 1768 but actually much older. It is a sad tale of unrequited love. Verse 3 goes like this:

> Oh he's titled Glenlogie
> Fan he is at hame,
> He's of the noble Gordons
> *Lord John is his name.*

And, after a chorus, Verse 4 continues:

> Oh he turned about *lichtly* (lightly)
> *As the Gordons dee aa* (all do).
> (Author's italics)

The Gordons continued to live in a light and lively fashion.

They provided the cavalry for Montrose's army in the so-called English Civil War and forfeited their lands as supporters of the Jacobite cause. Raising the Gordon Highlanders helped their rehabilitation, although the recruitment methods of the Duchess of Gordon caused tongues to wag.

Before they were disbanded, on the big table in the Officers' Mess of the Gordon Highlanders was a large silver centrepiece of the Duchess of Gordon, side-saddle on her pony and with a shilling in her lips, kissing one of her loyal tenants. By this action the besotted young man 'took the King's shilling' and was enlisted.

In his short poem *"Bydand"* Charles Murray (aka 'Hamewith') has the voice of 'a poor country lass', in sorrow.

> There's a yellow thread in the Gordon plaid,
>   But it binds na my love an' me;…
>
> For my lad would 'list: when a Duchess kiss't
>   He forgot a' the vows he made;
> An' he turned and took but ae lang, last look,
>   When the 'Cock o' the North' was played.
>
> Gin I were the Duke, I could nae mair look
>   Wi' love on my high-born dame;
> At a kilt or plaid I would hang my head,
>   An' think aye on my lady's shame.

(Bydand = biding = holding on = the regimental motto of the Gordon Highlanders, whose Gordon tartan was the Government tartan with a yellow thread through it. Cock o' the North was the regimental Quick March).

Rehabilitation was completed with the appointment of George Hamilton Gordon, the 4th Earl, as Prime Minister of the coalition government at the time of the Crimean War. Queen Victoria and Prince Albert were frequent visitors to Haddo House. The Balmoral Estate was leased to them until, in 1848, Albert acquired the lease from the 4th Earl.

As the Ulster Medical Journal reported: 'Four deaths in the space of ten years brought John Campbell Gordon to the peerage'. Plus some judicial proceedings. From 1881 to 1885 he represented the Queen as Lord High Commissioner to the General Assembly of the Church of Scotland. In 1886, as part of Gladstone's Third Ministry, he was appointed Lord Lieutenant of Ireland. Gladstone's First Home Rule Bill was defeated, the Liberal party was wrecked and Lord Gordon was out of a job.

From 1893 to 1898 he was Governor General of Canada, where he:

> ...transformed the role of Governor General from that of the aristocrat representing the King or Queen in Canada to a symbol representing the interests of all citizens.

He showed great acumen in buying a ranch in British Columbia, launching the commercial orchard industry of the Okanagon Valley. (In 1885 the Canadian Pacific Railway had completed the Canadian transcontinental rail link. Aberdeen must have recognised the similarity of some of the valleys of British Columbia to the apple-growing areas of Ireland).

In January 1906 the Liberals returned to power (under Campbell-Bannerman and, later, Asquith) with a huge majority. Lord Gordon was back in Ireland, where he was to serve as Lord Lieutenant (Viceroy) until January 1915.

Johnny Gordon was of the aristocracy. The family of **Ishbel Marjoribanks (1857-1939)** were Nouveaux Riches. Sir Dudley Coutts Marjoribanks was a brewing banker whose Brook House in Park Lane was a 'palace where…the staircase was a medley of mahogany and marble'. When Marjoribanks became the first Lord Tweedmouth in 1881 'the entertainments at this palace became more dazzling still'. He bought the huge estate of 19,186 acres at Guisachan, 23 miles south-west of Beauly, where he created the estate-village of Tomich and where the breed of Golden Retriever was developed and recognised. (PLATE 1a))

Ishbel received a well-rounded education in English, French, mathematics, history, and geography, and was such a good student that her teacher recommended she attend college. However, her father shared the widely held opinion that university was no place for a woman.

Instead, her education continued at home at her parents' social events, where she met the famous politicians of the day. This experience helped prepare her for a lifetime of political involvement.

It was at Guisachan that Johnnie Gordon dropped in unexpectedly and was spotted from the hall above by the 14 year old Ishbel as he went in to dinner. 'That's the one for me', she thought. They were married in St George's, Hanover Square, London in 1877.

Anne-Michelle Slater, Head of the Law School of Aberdeen University wrote in *Learning from the Lasses: Women of the Patrick Geddes Circle:*

> She and her husband, who was by now a regular at the House of Lords, shared a strong sense of duty, rooted in Christian philosophy and belief, as well as a love of the outdoor life – both typical of the

aristocracy at the time. They resolved to devote their lives to solid useful work, which should do something of good in the world.

They were a good team, described as 'contrasting, he bearded and small and polite, she disproportionately large, matronly and masterful'. Slater says:

> She apparently also had an aptitude for getting things just a little wrong; for interfering with things that had nothing to do with her and for an apparent inability to recognise a rebuff.

In old age Aberdeen and his wife jointly wrote a memoir called *We Twa'*, a reference to Burns's celebration of conjugal love, *Auld Lang Syne:*

> We twa hae run about the braes,
> > And pou'd the gowans fine;
> But we've wander'd mony a weary fit,
> > Sin auld lang syne.
> > > For auld lang syne, &c.

> We twa hae paidl'd in the burn,
> > Frae morning sun till dine;
> But seas between us braid hae roar'd,
> > Sin auld lang syne.
> > > For auld lang syne, &c.

Not many aristocratic couples could make such claims!

Their married life started at Haddo House, where the tenants turned out and escorted them over the last mile of the journey. Celebrations lasted a week, with a banquet for over 900 tenants and their wives. Haddo House was a William Adam house of 1732. The Gordons initiated 'an opulent remodelling'. The house was renovated, extended and altered. Sir Edward Hamilton's diary entry for 24 October 1882 included – 'Aberdeen is said to have spent £100,000 on Haddo House in Adamesque alterations and decorations…it makes a fine pile.' (PLATE 1b) The estates were licked into shape and Ishbel's 'talent for good simple and practical ideas to improve the lives of others' started at Haddo – with excellent organisation.

> She took a keen interest in the education, development and even entertainment of their servants, providing 'hops', special holiday meals, followed by treats such as magic lantern shows. She started a Household Club, with regular classes. A singing class was led by the head forester, a carving class by the governess, a drawing class by the nurse and a home reading circle led by a neighbouring school master. There were fortnightly social evenings of music, singing, recitation and short lectures. The Aberdeens usually attended these meetings.

At the same time, the Aberdeens kept their place in London society. Ishbel regarded teas, balls and parties as bearable as giving the opportunity for 'influencing for good' the people of wealth and power in Britain.

However, the Aberdeens did face ridicule from society and Barrie satirised their radical notions in *The Admirable Crichton*, although he apologised later. Gossip had it that they ate with the servants, so that Queen Victoria had to make enquiries as to whether this was true.

At home they continued their good works, endowing a cottage hospital, providing an institute for the education of young men in Methlick and arranging for penny hot lunches for the school children throughout their estate area.

Lady Aberdeen began to focus on female needs,
…with working parties where farmers' wives and their daughters met

to sew for the destitute, have tea and listen while a worthwhile book was read aloud.

This led to the creation of the Onwards and Upwards Association, designed for servant girls, who took postal courses on various subjects such as history, geography, bible studies, literature, domestic science, needlework and knitting – with prizes and certificates being awarded annually. Eventually it had 115 branches and 8280 members across Scotland before it was absorbed into the Scottish Mothers Union.

As Slater says:

> Lady Aberdeen was clearly emerging as the organiser and implementer of the union and although she had lavish personal tastes she appeared to be a generous benefactor. Her husband was also generous, but somewhat impractical and whimsical in his schemes for the estate, such as a branch railway through their properties.
>
> Politics, for both of them, however, provided focus, excitement and drama; and by 1880 Haddo House was regarded as a hotbed of Liberalism.

When her husband was first invited to be Viceroy, Ishbel was horrified and refused to cross the Irish Sea. She was aware of the terrible poverty, appalling living conditions and disease in the urban areas, the miserable state of agriculture post-Famine, particularly in the West, and the turbulent nature of Irish politics. Nevertheless, in the first period in Ireland, despite its short duration, she threw herself wholeheartedly into projects, schemes and plans for the development of Ireland and its people.

The story is told of the grand dinner at the Viceregal Lodge where Ishbel's neighbour opined that there were only two Home Rulers in the room – her 'and the wine waiter over there'.

At first she particularly focussed on Irish craft skills. She used the opportunity of the Women's Home Industries section of the Edinburgh International Exhibition of 1886 to exhibit Irish lace, embroideries, poplin and other handicrafts. Lady Aberdeen sourced these from all over Ireland, wrote up the catalogue, with details about the origins of each craft and the role each had in the economy of the island.

A garden party was held at the Viceregal Lodge in Dublin, where all the guests had to wear clothes of Irish materials, including the children, who had to wear fancy dress. On the Viceregal tennis courts an exhibition was held in which Irish manufacturers displayed their goods and milliners, tailors and dressmakers were invited to view the show. The men had to wear white flannels or homespun suits and soft hats. The ladies had to wear linen, laces, embroideries, poplins and woollens.

The garden party caught the imagination of the public and the Dublin newspapers. Lady Aberdeen became the Chairman of a newly formed Association of Irish Industries and a founder member of the Mansion House Ladies Committee.

In Canada the Governor-Generalship was a successful period for the Aberdeens, with many achievements and developments. There she founded the Victorian Order of Nurses and the National Council of Women in Canada. In 1893 she was elected President of the International Council for Women, a position she was to hold until 1936.

But Ireland was not forgotten. She continued to promote Irish industries abroad. Sales of Irish industries were instituted twice a year and depots for distribution of Irish goods were established in London and Dublin. For the World's Craft Fair in Chicago in 1893 an Irish Village was created - one of the main financial successes of the exhibition - resulting in a good deal of interest and orders for Irish goods in America.

'Our Chicago correspondent' of the *Londonderry Sentinel* of 18 July 1893 gives this description of 'Independence Day at the Irish Village':

From early morning till near midnight the walls of Donegal Castle echoed with the sounds of the Irish pipes, the strains of Irish melodies, the clang of the step of the Irish clog dance. Thousands of Irishmen passed through the old St Lawrence Gate of Drogheda into the village, drawn thither by the desire to hear the sweet Gaelic tongue, to stand on Irish soil, to sit in the chair of Daniel O'Connell to gaze on the features of Ireland's present day liberator, Gladstone, and to see the exhibits of Irish art, industry, history and antiquity which Mrs Ernest Hart has gathered together in the picturesque little village in the Midway Plaisance. In the afternoon the dancing and music ceased for a time, and Mrs Ernest Hart gave an address to a large and attentive audience on the lessons of Irish history taught by the Village; how the history of Ireland can be traced step by step in the Village by the representations of Druidical pillar stones, Ogham stones, round towers, Celtic crosses, Celtic illuminations, the castle and gateway, and the gallery of portraits of great Irishmen, right from the beginning when Ireland was crystallising out of chaos, as shown in the reproduction of the wishing chair of the Giant's Causeway, to the last act, as shown in the pictures of Gladstone bringing in the Home Rule Bill. No phase of Irish life and art and history has been forgotten in this representation of Ireland at Chicago, and it is highly appreciated by Irishmen, who gather day after day to hear Mrs Hart tell her stories of the saints who painted the illuminated books of the 7th century, who built the round towers, who made Ireland great in the past, and of the efforts now being made to make her happy and prosperous in the present. The dedication of the Village by the Catholic Primate of Chicago was the occasion of a great Irish demonstration, and the Irish are arranging other great celebration days at the Irish Village to evidence their appreciation of Mrs Hart's labours and the representation of their country at Chicago.

When the Aberdeens returned to Ireland for their second spell they were still determined to do good, although there had been some distinct changes since their last occupancy of the Vice-Regal Lodge in 1886. To quote Slater:

> There had been a social and legal transformation, with the transfer to tenants of much of the land previously held by landlords. This gave a new sense of pride and personal independence to the former tenants. It also appeared to reinforce a fresh awareness of Irish culture. The terrible living conditions and extreme poverty in the towns and particularly in Dublin city, however, led to serious discontent. Unemployment was higher than ever and the slums were more overcrowded and unsanitary. Infant mortality was extremely high and tuberculosis had joined the other diseases of typhoid, typhus, scarlet fever and smallpox that were rife at that time.

> Politically it was complex, with Home Rule being both promoted and opposed, particularly in Ulster, all with the backdrop of the rise of Sinn Fein. There was also a growing unrest among workers supported by strong union leaders.

> It was into this difficult and changing Ireland that the Aberdeens came, but by this time Lady Aberdeen had an excellent track record in organisation and leadership and was well equipped to do more than wear and promote Irish fashion.

This time she focused on healthcare and social well-being. Health and hygiene came first. Her crusade against tuberculosis was truly remarkable. In 1907 she headed up The Women's National Health Association of Ireland - one of the medical organizations that were dedicated to treating and preventing tuberculosis and improving children's health. She was the driving force behind the foundation of the Peamount and Rosslare Sanatoria and the Sutton Preventorium. At the same time, a spectrum of support activities was set up – aftercare in the home, Child Welfare Work, Infant Mortality Work, Babies' Clubs, School Children's Dental Clinics and the Maintenance of Visiting Nurses. Over time came the provision of playgrounds and school gardens, the organisation and staging of exhibitions, including Health and Housing, Child Welfare, and Food, which toured Ireland as part of the intensive TB campaign. Health Literature and Health Lectures were sent around the country, illustrated by lantern slides. Meals for School Children and Folk Dancing enriched the diet and provided healthy exercise.

Despite all this, Lady Aberdeen was in despair when, in a speech, she asked:

> What is the point of spending money in fighting TB if sufferers come back from sanatoriums to crowded unhealthy dwellings? What's the use of rescuing children if their Mothers have to live in overcrowded, contaminated dwellings?

Although she had been quite popular during her first stint in Ireland, she had faced a different reception upon her return. By 1906 nationalist sentiment had increased significantly in Ireland, and her ties to Britain were held against her. Furthermore, her determination to have her way meant that she was not always sensitive to the Irish perspective. What had seemed to be likeable patrician eccentricity was now seen as Imperialist interference, while she herself saw that craft works and health provision were merely tinkering with Irish problems. Something more fundamental was needed.

Lady Aberdeen began to explore the wider ideas of town planning and civic survey and found inspiration and practical support from **Patrick Geddes (1854-1932)**. (PLATE 2a)

Turn by turn - and even simultaneously – Patrick Geddes was a botanist, economist, sociologist, producer of pageants, public lecturer, writer of verse, art critic, publisher, civic reformer, town planner, Victorian moralist, provocative agnostic and academic revolutionary. (He was Sir Patrick Geddes for only 52 days, dying in Montpellier from an infection picked up in London at the time of his investiture.)

In his time he was internationally influential. (See Appendix 2) After his death he fell into some obscurity, but was rediscovered in the 1970s and is now regarded as a kind of secular saint of the environmental movement.

On the other hand, Alex Law, Professor of Sociology at Abertay University, Dundee has described Geddes as 'a failed sociologist'.

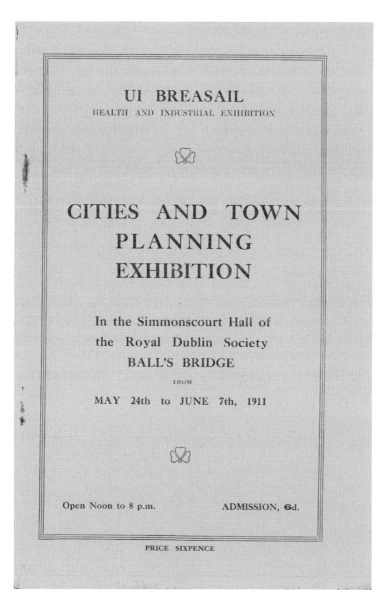

FIG 1
Cities and Town Planning Exhibition Catalogue, Dublin 1911
(Sir Patrick Geddes Memorial Trust)

Geddes had prepared an important City and Town Planning Exhibition for Chelsea in 1910. After touring Great Britain it was brought over to Dublin by the Aberdeens, to the Royal Dublin Society's premises at Ballsbridge, and was backed up by a series of lectures, by Geddes and other leading figures. 160,000 attended in the first two weeks, after which the exhibition was transferred to Trinity College, Dublin, backed up by a lecture series under the auspices of the Royal Institute of Public Health Congress. (FIG 1)

For Geddes, parks and gardens were more than merely recreational. In an interview for the *Freeman's Journal* he said:

> I would venture upon things that are simple, easy and obvious and things that everyone would approve of. I would tackle things like mending and cleaning and brightening of derelict corners and tumble down houses, and especially the letting out of little bits of garden, that the casual labourer in the workhouse should be absorbed by your garden. I would have two types of garden, small patches in the crowded areas and the larger gardens where the population is not so crowded.

Community gardens could also be a means of bringing about change in a non-controversial fashion. Local groups working towards a common end, like a garden, would learn how to get more complex things done – such as outwitting bureaucracy or outflanking conservatism.

When Geddes returned to Scotland his daughter Norah, a landscape architect and gardener, stayed behind to start a programme of 'greening the urban environment' of Dublin, where it was estimated that there were 2,000 derelict sites, ripe for improvement.

In 1911 the Housing and Town Planning Association of Ireland was formed, to fight for better housing and public spaces to address the prevalent poverty. Lady Aberdeen served as the

Association's first president.

In search of a good photograph of Lady Aberdeen I turned to Geddes's papers. In the 1950s Patrick Geddes's Outlook Tower in Edinburgh ('...the world's first sociological laboratory') was in a bad way and Arthur Geddes sold a large quantity of archival material to Dr Thomas Lyon of the Royal Technical College in Glasgow. Lyon gave the archive to the Department of Architecture, it passed on to the Department of Urban and Regional Planning and then to the Library of what was, by then, Strathclyde University. The Patrick Geddes Archive is vast (the Index consists of six weighty volumes). One marvels at the industry of the great man! The contents are very varied in quality and width but I found an entry which looked promising.

An electronic copy arrived from Strathclyde of 'The Work of the Women's National Health Association of Ireland' by 'The Countess of Aberdeen'. 43 pages of good, solid, factual reporting, with 2 graphs and 21 photographs, three of them featuring the Countess with an imposing hat. She is one of two women members of the Viceregal Milk Commission and is weighing the baby at the Ballymacarret Babies' Club in Dublin.

The report is dated 1912 and clearly was sent to Geddes as it refers to him, particularly in relation to the 1911 Dublin Exhibition (which transferred to Belfast) and 'Garden Playgrounds'.

The best thing to do with this report would be to publish it in its entirety. But this would throw this whole account out of balance, so I have limited myself to headings in Appendix 1. Four illustrations and a few quotable notes also follow, giving a flavour of the WNHA's achievement. It is great, inspiring reporting. So sad that all her efforts should have been negated by politics!

Very early in the history of the Association it was perceived that the road to success lay in attacking the problem from every standpoint, and that to carry on a Tuberculosis Campaign really meant a campaign in the interests of good health, and included the education of Mothers in the care of their children from their birth; the watching over the interests of children through infancy, childhood and youth; the education of the public generally as to the importance of the selection of nourishing food and its preparation; the urgent necessity of fresh air, and healthy surroundings of the home, as well as good and sanitary housing.

In 1864 the deaths per1000 in Scotland were 3.6, in England 3.3 and in Ireland 2.4. By 1911 the order had changed and the figures were now Ireland 2.2, Scotland 1.8, England 1.4 – although Ireland had recorded a sharp drop from 1907.

In 1908 the Association shared the first prize of 1,000 dollars with the COS of New York as the two voluntary Societies who had done the most effective work against Tuberculosis.

In 1909, however, The Countess of Aberdeen, when visiting New York, received a very generous offer from Mr Robert J Collier of New York…whereby he undertook to place in her hands £3,000 to be paid in yearly instalments for the purpose of providing a Memorial in Ireland of his father, who was so well-known and so deservedly popular in Ireland.

The P F Collier Memorial Dispensary for the Prevention of Tuberculosis was the result. In its first year 1176 persons attended. It was purchased by the City of Dublin in 1911.

A great scarcity of milk…contamination and infection. Vice-Regal Milk Commission set up. Milk depots opened.

Members of the Viceregal Milk Commission

FIG 2
Members of the Viceregal Milk Commission
(University of Strathclyde)

The housing conditions of the 1,176 persons attending the Dispensary may be judged by the following notes:

Persons living in Lodging Houses   12
Patients belonging to families occupying one room   676
"   "   two rooms   278
"   "   three rooms   96
"   "   four rooms   74
"   "   five or more rooms   40

The majority of families living in one room select the top-back because of its cheapness in spite of the fact that every drop of water for family use must be carried up four or five stories. Cellars are also in demand.

Milk Depot at Limerick.

FIG 3
Milk Depot at Limerick
(University of Strathclyde)

The Travelling Health Exhibition started as a Tuberculosis Exhibition and has developed into a Health Exhibition...in Ireland...invitation to England and Scotland, three months in Wales.

The Travelling Health Caravan.

FIG 4
The Travelling Health Caravan
(University of Strathclyde)

"Garden Playgrounds" are made out of derelict sites of the town's crowded quarters, some of them open to the street, some entirely shut in by the surrounding houses.

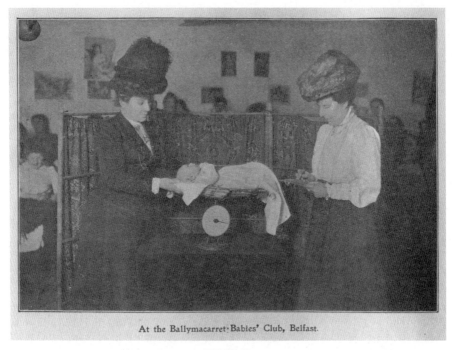

At the Ballymacarret Babies' Club, Belfast.

FIG 5
At the Ballymacarett Babies' Club, Belfast
(University of Strathclyde)

Ui Breasail...lasted for a fortnight...and was visited by over 172,000 people. It brought in over £11,800 to the Central Association and over £600 to the local branches.'

Geddes was back again in 1914, as a guest of the Aberdeens, masterminding, with Lady Aberdeen, on behalf of the Housing and Town Planning Association of Ireland, another Civic Exhibition in Dublin. Geddes had the great advantage that, as an outsider and a loose cannon, he could go into places and meet people like striking Trade Unionists which the Aberdeens could not, because of protocol.

This exhibition was to be for all the people and, instead of establishment locations like RDS or Trinity College it was staged in the Linen Hall Barracks, in Henrietta Street, in north Dublin, in an area of extreme poverty.

The Exhibition opened on 15 July 1914 with a lavish ceremony. There was a civic pageant at which Lady Aberdeen was presented with a golden key with which she performed the opening ceremony. *The Irish Times* addressed her in the following terms:

> You are not likely to be forgotten in this city for your devotion, unfaltering, resistant, restless, ever-working for the welfare, the health and the prosperity of the Irish people.

The Exhibition was a great success, with displays provided by planners, individuals and Government departments. There were displays and demonstrations of poultry rearing and bee-keeping, of cookery, printing and bookbinding and of useful crafts like carpentry, tailoring and wire mattress making (more hygienic!) Out of doors agricultural skills were displayed, including manuring techniques and from Belfast was brought a municipal abattoir. After dark the latest methods of street lighting were shown.

There were free medical and dental inspections for school children, folk dancing, and the usual 'sideshows' for such an occasion. The WHNA ladies served light meals in the tea gardens.

Patrick Geddes, of course, presided over the Summer School of Civics while Lady Aberdeen proposed that a civic survey be undertaken. The Lord Lieutenant felt so strongly on the subject that he offered a prize for the best civic plan,

> …with the special object of furnishing and convenient housing for the working classes around the city.

All was going well till, one evening after dinner, Geddes was declaiming:

I urge not only that the collections in the Linen Hall be preserved permanently, but that the re-planning scheme which wins the Viceroy's prize can be carried out courageously and beginning this very summer.

Later that same evening, Lord Aberdeen, having received a telegram, broke the news that war had started. It was 4 August 1914.

That was the end of the Exhibition, as the Linen Hall was required as a barracks, and then a military hospital. On the last day, a Sunday, Ishbel was on her own in the Exhibition when a mob from the slums outside broke in and looted the place, carrying away tables and chairs and much else. Lord Leverhulme had contributed a model of his planned village of Port Sunlight but was not discomfited by the looters. He thought that it would be no bad thing if one of his model houses ended up on someone's mantelpiece as an example of what they should be striving for!

Geddes was already under contract to go off to India, where he spent the war planning fifty cities for the peace to follow. He was joined by Alastair, his older son. His Cities Exhibition – a major source of income for him – went out separately in the *Clan Grant*, which had the misfortune to meet the German commerce raider *Emden*, which sent ship and exhibition to the bottom of the Indian Ocean. It was 1926 before Geddes received £2,054 compensation for the loss of his Exhibition.

With the coming of war 175,000 of the Irish National Volunteers left to join up, leaving 13,500 behind to subvert actively the British presence in Ireland. Lady Aberdeen's plans for planning and for Dublin, inspired by Patrick Geddes, were allowed to run into the sand. After the war there was no time for anything which smacked of the imperialist past.

Lord Aberdeen's Lord Lieutenancy ended in January 1915, and on 17th February 1915 The Lord Wimborne, first cousin of Winston Churchill took over. Aberdeen may have been too conciliatory towards the Nationalist faction, whereas Wimborne's style was confrontational. He fought in the Boer War, went into politics as a Conservative, then followed Churchill into the Liberal party in 1904. In WWI he served in the 10th (Irish) Division, which was one of the first of Kitchener's New Army Divisions (the so-called Pals Battalions). In the Easter Rising of 1916 77 of the rebels were killed, as against 145 British military and police. Wimborne enforced martial law during the Easter Rising and refused to offer his resignation thereafter. Under pressure from the government he did resign and was then re-appointed.

Almost immediately after Lord Aberdeen's losing his post, he and Ishbel travelled to America on a fund-raising mission for Irish charitable causes. They hoped to reach their target in six months, but it took them two years. The main beneficiaries were the Women's National Health Association and the Peamount Sanatorium. In 1916 Johnny was created 1st Marquess of Aberdeen and Temair (in Ireland) and Ishbel became a Marchioness.

They built for their retirement a beautiful new house in Glentanar. They worked on We Twa'. Valentine of Dundee, well-known for their postcards, published in 1929 *Jokes cracked by Lord Aberdeen* (PLATE 2b)). It is not every eminent politician whose wit and wisdom have become a cult classic. Here is the Foreword.

In the Realm of Wit and Humour, Lord Aberdeen is a name to conjure with. All the kindly geniality of the North comes out in his rich repertoire of stories, and here the Publishers have pleasure in introducing to a wider public a few Gems from his collection.

John Finnemore, in his Introduction to the 2013 edition, writes:

I find myself oddly protective of the author. I like that he enjoyed cracking jokes. I like that despite being a Marquess and a former Lieutenant Governor of Ireland he didn't think it was beneath him to publish a book of them, and I quite like, ooh, at least six of his jokes. So, here's to John Hamilton-Gordon. Long may he have them rolling in the aisles…

Let the reader make the judgment. One of the shorter stories follows. Even in the twenty-first century I find this quite amusing – and so do others in my circle.

THE DOCTOR"S CURE

A Doctor on being called in to see one of his patients
informed the good lady of the house:
'What your husband wants is complete rest;
and so I have prescribed a sleeping draught.'
'Very well, doctor, and when shall I give it to him?'
'Oh don't give it to *him*, take it yourself' he replied.

Johnny Aberdeen's retirement was not untroubled. His business ventures in Canada and other investments were affected by the Wall Street crash. By the time he died in 1934 the 75,000 acres of family property held in 1872 had shrunk to 15,000. In 1974, David Gordon, the 4th Marquess, left Haddo House and its garden to the care of the National Trust for Scotland.

The Marchioness, however, could not be idle. From having been an irritating Lady Aberdeen she had become the Meddling Marchioness. Although not a suffragette she continued trying to improve the position of women in society. She was the first woman to be made an honorary member of the British Medical Association. She continued to serve as the president of the International Council of Women until 1936. In 1931, she organized and presented to the General Assembly of the Church of Scotland a petition of 336 women calling for women to be ordained to the ministry, diaconate and eldership of the Kirk. This resulted in a special commission, which recommended only that women should be ordained as deacons. It was not until 1968 that the Church of Scotland passed acts allowing women to become elders or enter the ministry. Ishbel did not live to see this modest revolution, having died of a heart attack on 18 April 1939 at Gordon House in Rubislaw, Aberdeen.

The focus now switches to the Province of Ulster, nine counties in the north of Ireland, to Donegal and Londonderry. England spent centuries sporadically taking over parts of Ireland and 'settling' them. Most history books ignore the fact that, for most of Elizabeth's golden reign there was almost continual trouble with the Irish nobility, from time to time erupting into bloody war.

In 1595 Hugh O'Neill, Earl of Tyrone and Red Hugh O'Donnell, Earl of Tyrconnel rose against the English, at first with some success but ending with 'The Flight of the Earls' from Donegal in 1607. In 1608 a revolt by Sir Cahir O'Doherty was crushed. Half a million acres of 'profitable' land were confiscated and 'undertakers' were entrusted with settling the land with English and Scottish settlers with English law and language and the Protestant religion.

Meanwhile, in Scotland, when James VI, King of Scots, attained adulthood he set about taking control of the Highlands and Islands. On Elizabeth of England's death he assumed control of both sides of the troubled Borders and set about clearing them up, setting up a Border Commission. So ferocious did the pacification of the Borders become that in 1606 the King observed that it was 'savouring altogidder of barbarisme'. Many of the malcontents were sent to the gallows and more were outlawed. Some fled to Ulster while large numbers were 'resettled' in what is generally known as the Plantation of Ulster.

For example, Crozier is not a common surname in Northern Ireland, but an examination of the pre-mobile telephone directory for Northern Ireland shows a remarkable clustering of Croziers in County Fermanagh, near Enniskillen. Over in Scotland there is a similar cluster of Croziers in and around Hawick in the Borders, descended from the families loyal enough not to be despatched, like the 300, to Fermanagh.

In the North West the Crown persuaded the merchants of the City of London to undertake the task. An early settlement by the Foyle called Derry (*Doire* = woodlands) was fortified to become the City of Londonderry and the lands to the east became County Londonderry. The plantation was managed by a company called, after 1660, the Honourable the Irish Society, or simply the Irish Society – which still has premises in the city. By 1613 the lands around Limavady and Dungiven in the Roe valley still had some patches of 'native freeholders', with names like O'Cahan and O'Mulligan, but these were surrounded by Church lands and the lands of the London Companies of Grocers, Fishmongers, Haberdashers and Skinners.

Evidence for this settlement can be picked up from a perusal of Sheet 7 (Londonderry) of the *Ordnance Survey of Northern Ireland* where we can see adjacent place names like Eglinton (Scottish) and Ballykelly (Irish), Dowland and Drumaderry, Stoneyfalls and Dunnamanagh. In County Londonderry, outside the towns eight 'cricket grounds' are marked, beside villages and in the open countryside. West of the Foyle, in Donegal and the Republic of Ireland there are none. In the Waterside suburb of Derry is a small development called Brigade, named after a local club with obvious military connections. The street names are the names of the Brigade players of the 'Sixties, when the estate was built.

A conspiracy to seize Derry and the other English forts and to extirpate the English planters was thwarted in 1615 but did not lessen the mistrust of the planters of the native Irish. Children from Christ's Hospital and other poor children were brought over to be apprentices and servants, so 'that the inhabitants were to be prohibited from taking Irish apprentices'.

After James VII and II was removed from the British throne most of Ireland remained loyal to him. When his forces moved to take over Londonderry a raft of symbols was created which can still be seen in city murals and on commemorative parades. As the royal forces approached, the twelve *Prentice Boys* closed the gates. A lengthy siege followed, when the cry was *No Surrender. The Maiden City* was relieved when the *Mountjoy* broke the boom and sailed up the river.

William of Orange landed at *Carrickfergus* and met James's army at the River Boyne, where *King Billy on his white horse* rode through the waters of the river to victory. From that day *Remember 1690* has been the slogan and parades of bands have played the stirring tunes of *Derry's Walls, The Protestant Boys* and *On the Green Grassy Slopes of the Boyne* (these are now banned!) and banners have recorded resistance to absolute and capricious monarchy.

There is a problem of nomenclature. What's in a name? The title page of Robert Simpson's 1847 history of the city illustrates the problem. His book is *The Annals of Derry showing...and thence of The City of Londonderry'*. What are we to call this divided city?

Officialdom – the UK Government, the Ordnance Survey, the Geological Survey, the Census, even the *AA Road Atlas Ireland* – all call it Londonderry. Royal Mail avoids the issue by having only one major postcode area in the North – Belfast - but there are two postcode areas in Londonderry – BT46 and BT47.

However, the airport is called 'City of Derry'. The road signs of the North West have had the London painted out by the brave boys, leaving '...derry'. Derry City, the leading local football team, have their ground at Brandywell west of the river and play in the Irish League while, when Sinn Fein came into power, the city was democratically renamed City of Derry. Atlases published in the Republic not only call the city Derry, but do not show the border. So it was quite simple, really. Londonderry equals Protestant and Unionist, City of Derry means Catholic and Republican.

Gerry Anderson, an entertaining local disk jockey, noting that the form Derry/Londonderry was in common use, coined the term 'Stroke City', a clever reference to the hybrid title, but also to the high level of heart disease, partly related to the high level of stress during the Troubles. President Clinton looked to have sorted it all out when he talked about the City of Derry in the County of Londonderry.

However, it soon became clear that, underneath the political posturing, there was an undercurrent, especially among the older people, that refused, regardless of political affiliation, to waste valuable time with a polysyllabic title for their town. So Derry it is still, in common parlance. Perhaps we should be guided by Lady Aberdeen herself, who, according to the Londonderry Sentinel, on July 19th 1893 talked of Derry and then – 5 lines of newspaper report later - referred to Londonderry.

PLATE 1a)
Memorial Plaque to
Ishbel's Parents

PLATE 1b) Haddo House, home of the Gordons

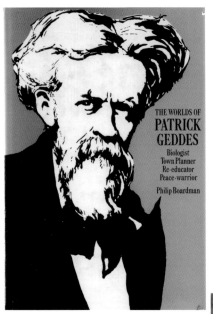

PLATE 2a)
Patrick Geddes - polymath

PLATE 2b)
Bestseller of 1922

PLATE 3a) The Fountain seen from Derry's Walls

PLATE 3b) Tillie and Henderson's factory, now demolished

PLATE 4a) Hogg and Mitchell's, now converted into apartments

PLATE 4b) 'Hands across the Divide', a powerful symbol

For many years Londonderry was a classic example of political gerrymandering. The city was divided into three wards, each electing three members to the City council. The smallest ward had about 5,000 voters and comprised the walled City, with the Church of Ireland cathedral, and the adjacent Fountain district of factories and industrial housing. All solidly Unionist and Protestant. (PLATE 3a))

Across the river was the Waterside, with about 15,000 voters. This had its factories and associated workers housing and, although it had a Catholic Republican element, was still comfortably Unionist and Protestant.

Back on the west side of the Foyle and surrounding the City's walls, were the Bogside and Creggan, with the Roman Catholic cathedral and a couple of lately established factories. Here there were about 35,000 voters, solidly Catholic and Republican, and maintained thus by local authority housing policies.

The end result was that, as long as the boundaries were unchanged, whatever the number of votes cast, the council would always be Unionist and Protestant.

Donegal is different and difficult. 8km off the Inishowen coast is Inishtrahull, the island with the oldest rocks in Ireland, 1700 million years old, long before there was any life on Earth. Donegal is a mass of ancient rock, folded, twisted and metamorphosed, given a south-west to north-east trend during the Caledonian mountain-building period and more resembling the southern Highlands and islands of Scotland than the lands east of the Foyle. There the rocks are no earlier than the Old Red Sandstone and Carboniferous (a mere 350 million years old) and over much of Ulster are capped by the Tertiary basalts associated with more recent Alpine mountain-building. Over the last million years Donegal was a major ice centre, with valley glaciers and local mountain ice caps.

The result was a landscape of old, hard rocks which did not break down to give good soil. Although not particularly high, the mountains were scraped bare and separated by some of the boggiest peat bogs in Europe (for example, Poisoned Glen). In 1837 Lewis's *Topographical Dictionary* described northwest Donegal as:

> ...a dreary wilderness of rugged mountain wastes and heaths broken in the west into abrupt rocky heights...unsuitable for either grazing or tillage.

Reinforced by a wet and windy climate, this was never to be a rich agricultural area and for many years its main export was people.

Despite Percy French's nostalgia, Donegal in the 19th century was a troubled place. It had shared the potato blight, the famine and mass emigration with the rest of west Ireland. There was a sheep war and evictions. There were exploitative landlords, local as well as absentee. Young children were exported as labourers to the richer lands of Tyrone and Londonderry. Seasonal workers migrated to the Scottish lowlands and others sought their fortunes further afield, never to return, in mainland Britain, the United States, Canada and Australia.

A feature of Irish literature of the gritty kind was the gombeenman, who ruled the local economy. 'Gombeen – a money-lender, a profiteer. {Hiberno-English, from Irish *gaimbin*)' says the *Concise Ulster Dictionary*. The gombeenman controlled credit by such practices as demanding payment of interest in advance and exacting payment in kind at his prices. Perhaps understandably, there was in Donegal 'an embedded reluctance to pay either county cess' (land tax) 'or rates'.

Arthur Balfour (1848-1930) is best known as the Foreign Secretary under Lloyd George who issued the Balfour Declaration in

1917, promising a homeland to the Jewish people under certain conditions – which have not been observed. 'A brilliant debater, he was bored by the mundane tasks of party management'.

He served an apprenticeship as Chief Secretary for Ireland. As a Conservative he opposed Home Rule and state intervention. Nevertheless he is credited with having suppressed agrarian unrest whilst taking measures against absentee landlords. The McKinley tariffs in the United States had devastated the cottage industries and Balfour arranged for contracts of knitted socks for the army to be placed in the county. The knitters were paid 2s 6d (12.5p) a dozen, almost twice the price paid by the local agents, shopkeepers and gombeenmen.

Better communications, internally as well as with the outside world, were seen as critical for any development in the county. Although the big landowners could be expected to invest in schemes which benefited their own estates, a network could not have been financed from the savings of the impoverished local people. Balfour, conscious of the evictions and suffering, introduced a railway act in 1889, a land act in 1891 and set up a Congested Districts Board in 1891. – all:

...designed to relieve the recurrent cycles of poverty and violence... and make Ireland into a peaceful, stable society.

Under the railway act the government bore £1,554,000 (£155 million in 2019 prices) of the £1,850,000 expended on railway development in Donegal up to 1903.

Percy French (1854-1920) was an Inspector of Drains who became a celebrated singer, composer and performer in at least three continents. My preference is for the comic songs, *Phil the Fluter's Ball, Slattery's Mounted Fut, McBreen's Heifer* and the like. *Abdallah*

Bulbul Ameer (Words and Music by Percy French) was a great favourite with rugby clubs in my day. His sentimental songs are a little too sweet for me, but I recognize the power and pathos of *The Mountains of Mourne, Come back Paddy Reilly* and *Gortnamona*. An appealing feature of his songs is that they are placed in real and recognisable places.

The Emigrant's Letter starts:

Dear Danny, I'm takin' the pen in me hand
To tell ye we're just out o' sight o' the land
In the grand Allan Liner I'm sailing in style
But I'm sailing away from the Emerald Isle
And a long sort o' sigh seemed to come from us all
As the waves hid the last bit of ould Donegal,
Oh it's well to be you that is takin' yer tay
Where they're cuttin' the corrun in Creeshla the day.

and goes on to bewail the good people, however poor and simple, he is leaving behind.

When I was investigating the North West in the 1890s both the *Derry Journal* and the *Londonderry Sentinel* carried on the front page an advertisement for the Allan Line. The big ship would anchor in deep water off Moville in Lough Foyle. Would-be emigrants would board lighters in Derry, be taken down the Lough and transshipped for the great adventure in the New World.

After World War I a plebiscite in Ulster resulted in three counties, Donegal, Cavan and Monaghan, going into the Irish Free State, capital Dublin, and the remaining six counties forming Northern Ireland, capital Belfast. County Donegal was now in a strange condition. Most British counties are, in geographical terms, core-periphery models. In County Tyrone, for example, Omagh, with its cathedral, sits in the middle and all the roads from the towns and villages of the county lead to it, like the spokes of a wheel (FIG 6).

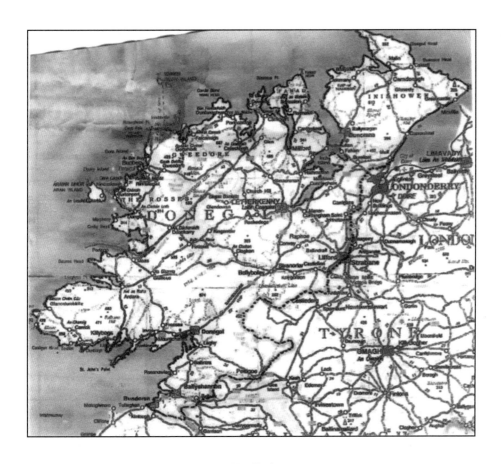

FIG 6
County Donegal and Derry (Frank Sweeney)
(NB – The Border near Ballyshannon in the south
is incorrectly shown)

But Donegal is a network. The topography makes it impossible for a central focus to develop. Settlement is dispersed around the coast and no one settlement can dominate. Donegal Town is quite small and at one end of the county. For most people in Donegal the most convenient places are Derry and, to a lesser extent, Strabane, across the border. Donegal feels quite isolated from Dublin, a feeling made more obvious by the fact that the only road to Dublin which does not pass through Northern Ireland is in a corridor 8 km across between Ballyshannon and Donegal Bay.

Nothing exemplifies this situation better than a consideration of the railway map around 1909. In Londonderry there were four railway termini, two on either side of the Foyle. In the Waterside the Belfast and Northern Counties line on the standard Irish Gauge of 5 feet 3 inches went off to Coleraine, Belfast and, eventually, Dublin. The same company operated a short line along the east side of the Foyle to Strabane in 1900.

West of the Foyle the Londonderry and Lough Swilly penetrated into Donegal, one line going to Letterkenny, the second largest town in Donegal (1883), with a branch traversing the Inishowen peninsula through Buncrana to Cardonagh in 1901. From 1903 the Letterkenny and Burtonport Extension Railway penetrated westwards to the Atlantic Ocean at Burtonport.

The Great Northern (Ireland) ran up the west side of the Foyle to Strabane (1847) and on via Omagh to Dublin, and in 1909 it opened a link from Strabane to Letterkenny.

In Donegal proper the Finn Valley Railway ran from Strabane to Stranorlar (1863). From Stranorlar the West Donegal Railway would take one to Druminin (1882) and, from 1889, to Donegal Town. From Donegal Town the Donegal Railway Company ran westwards to Killybegs, an important fishing port and southwards to Ballyshannon (1903), where one could change to the Great Northern line from Bundoran to Enniskillen and on to Dublin. Another Donegal Railway Company line from Stranorlar ran for 24 miles (39 Km) to Glenties, twelve miles north of Killybegs, from 1895. These railways were all on narrow gauge (3 feet) and, when amalgamated, under the County Donegal Railways Joint Committee in 1909, formed – at 225 miles - the largest narrow gauge railway in the British Isles – and probably the one with the poorest hinterland! (FIG 7)

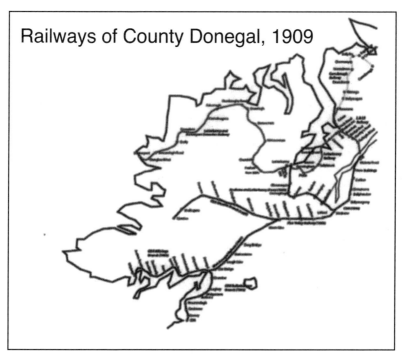

Railways of County Donegal, 1909

FIG 7
Railways of County Donegal, 1909
(Frank Sweeney)

From above, the railway network of the North West must have looked just like an octopus, the body being Londonderry from which seven or eight tentacles spread out.

Over in Scotland, from Edinburgh the A7 and the Borders Railway climb over the outliers of the Lammermuir and Moorfoot Hills and then follow the Gala Water down to Galashiels and the River Tweed. In the parish of Heriot, just south of the highest point, in the Scottish Borders (but which was earlier in Midlothian), is the farm of Crookston. Here was born **William Tillie (1823-1904)**. He learned the textile business in Glasgow before moving to Londonderry in 1851. His success was down to his early adoption of the newly invented sewing machine, to the coupling of rows of sewing machines to a steam engine as well as to other technological innovations.

This provided the springboard for half a century of rapid growth and another half-century of edgy prosperity. Tillie and Henderson's huge shirt factory (PLATE 3b) became the largest in the world, dominating the Craigavon Bridge over the Foyle, with a workforce of 4,500. Lady Aberdeen, on her 1893 visit:

> ...believed Lord Shaftesbury once, on visiting Mr Tillie's factory, thanked God that he had had an opportunity of seeing such work going on.

and in a final accolade Karl Marx was so impressed that he referenced it in *Das Kapital:*

> The shirt factory of Messrs Tillie at Londonderry . . . employs 1,000 operatives in the factory itself, and 9,000 people spread up and down the country and working in their houses.

Tillie's 'factory girls' were renowned for their enterprising, independent nature and the camaraderie on the factory floor. They were the first female workers in Ireland to become unionised and in 1891 they were admitted to the Derry Trades Council.

Tillie occupied an important place in Londonderry society and was made Lieutenant of the City of Londonderry. He was a major figure in First Derry Presbyterian Church and had many philanthropic outlets. Agnes, his wife, also involved herself in charitable enterprises, chief of which was her interest in providing nursing for the 'working classes'. As Vice-President and founding member of the Londonderry District Nursing Society she personally financed a fully equipped District Nurses Home in Great James Street (in the congested industrial area of the city).

FIG 8
William Tillie (1823-1904) in late 1890s
when he was Lieutenant for the City of Londonderry
(Courtesy Ted McQuilken)

My own acquaintance with the city began in 1949 when my father, my pal Eddie Wilson and I cycled round Northern Ireland, staying in Youth Hostels. Unfortunately, there was no hostel in Derry, so my visit was confined to a Saturday, when we cycled from east of Limavady, spent a few hours exploring in the city and then set off south to Learmount Castle at the foot of the Sperrin Mountains.

I was back again for a week at Easter in 1951. I had befriended a Derry boy at the Royal Technical College in Glasgow and he had stayed with us a few times. In return, I was invited over to Derry. The visit was not a success. The weather was execrable, I found the attitudes of my hosts difficult to take and my own social inadequacies were in evidence. (I have to record that, twenty years later, my former classmate was shot dead as he came out of church on a Sunday morning).

Jane McBride neé Walker (1910-2011) was one of a large family, the paterfamilias of which had a grocery business and small farm at 'the top of the Chapel Brae' in the Waterside of Londonderry. Known as Daisy, she married a local boy before the Second World War and together they lived in London, Wallasey, Worcester and Prestwick before settling in Edinburgh. When Jack retired Northern Ireland was in turmoil, so that it was another ten years before they were able to return to the Waterside, to Deanfield.

From the air the Limavady Road runs from Craigavon Bridge eastwards, roughly parallel with the railway line and the south shore of Lough Foyle. A straight street of about 100 metres goes off to the north and breaks off into two arms, ending above the railway. At the north-west end of the road was Deanfield House, residence of the Lord Mayor, behind impressive gate pillars. Round the outer sides of each branch was a series of individually designed 3-storey villas, while between two small fields were left. A dairy farmer in the

Creggan had those fields and grew potatoes and grain there. From time to time they were used to keep cattle overnight before they were sent off by train from the Waterside station.

After the Second World War, the section in the middle and the Deanfield House grounds were filled in with smaller houses – architect-designed Arts and Crafts villas and superior bungalows. Into one of the latter my in-laws moved. On one side was **Arthur Hogg,** Elder of the First Presbyterian Church and former principal and manager of Hogg and Mitchell, one of the last surviving shirt factories in Derry. On the other was the daughter of a judge. She went blind, was taken into Deanfield - by now a nursing home – where she died. Her place was taken by Aidan Mulvey, a (Catholic) pharmacist – a symbol of the population changes now going on. Another was the 'At Home' held on the occasion of Daisy's 100th birthday, when the visitors' book revealed that the guests split exactly fifty/fifty Catholic/Protestant and many were so pleased to have spoken for the first time to neighbours from 'the other side'.

Arthur's relatives still farm at Brotherstone, 4 km as the crow flies from Tillie's birthplace at Crookston. **David Cleghorn Hogg (1840-1914),** like Tillie, made his way to Derry, and he too prospered. The new five-storey factory he had built in 1898 was in Little James Street, near the city centre, and was described in 1970 as:

A five-storey honestly expressed functional shirt factory in red brick …The architect aimed to "sweep away allusions to pilasters and string courses, and let the factory rise up, big, airy, massive and modern." It certainly rose up big and massive.

So said the Ulster Architectural Heritage Society in *Historic Buildings…In and Near the City of Derry*. Unlike Tillie's, which was too big and too old to be saved, Hogg and Mitchell's has been restored and recycled as city centre Hogg and Mitchell Apartments. (PLATE 4a)

David Hogg was younger than Tillie, whose daughter Agnes wrote in 1872 from her finishing school in Dresden to Jane (Jenny) Cooke in Ramelton, Co Donegal, who was later to marry Hogg. Like Tillie, Hogg had his place in local society, but, unlike Tillie, did not quite fit in. As a body the millowners of Derry were solidly Unionist. Hogg was a Home Ruler and therefore persona non grata with much of the city's upper crust. In the fevered politics of the time one election slogan was: 'Hogg in the river with a knife in his liver'.

Like Tillie he became Lord Lieutenant of County Londonderry. He was also elected as a Liberal/Home Rule MP to Westminster, receiving the support of the Catholic clergy, despite his religion. Arthur reckoned that Westminster killed his grandfather. Attendance at Westminster meant a train to Belfast – overnight ferry to Heysham (where the steward made his frequent acquaintance) – train to London. Factor in winter gales and delays and even First Class must have seemed intolerable. He was the last Liberal MP elected in Ireland in a contested election.

Arthur, his grandson, was an excellent fellow, Every time I visited Daisy I would pop next door for an evening with the whisky. Arthur was born in British Columbia but at the age of two was brought back to Derry where he was to live with aunts. (He lived in three houses in Deanfield – but not all at the same time!) He went to Campbell College in Belfast where he was drum major in the pipe band and played the oboe in the school orchestra.

In the Second World War the Territorial Army unit in Londonderry was a Heavy Ack Ack (Anti-Aircraft) Artillery battalion and with them Arthur first defended Alexandria, then served with the

Eighth Army in North Africa and Italy, where he contracted rheumatic fever and had to be invalided home. Hard by the new dual carriageway between Derry and the airport can be seen a cluster of low, decaying concrete structures. They are all that can be seen of an underground command post from which the area could have been controlled and administered had County Londonderry been bombed flat or invaded by the Germans. Arthur served out his time as Officer Commanding this emergency facility.

After the war he went into the family business. Old ladies have told me what a fine figure of a man he was when he strode into the factory, calling out 'Good morning, girls'. In the Derry factories there was a definite stratification. The owners, management and skilled workers were almost all Protestant and male, while almost all who manned the looms and sewing machines were Catholic and female.

At that time there were still outworkers sewing collars on to shirts and Arthur's job was to go round Donegal with the unfinished shirts, picking up the finished ones and paying for them. He never ceased to wonder at the beautifully white products coming out of miserable hovels with no running water and full of peat smoke and dust.

Later he operated as sales manager, visiting big stores in the cities of Britain and most European capitals, before assuming control of Hogg and Mitchell, where it was his fate to manage its decline. There were times when he wondered whether he and his peers in the other factories had been exploiting their workers. I did my best to reassure him that they were probably paying the rate for the job, reminding him that the lower wages of the foreign competition was one of the factors in the collapse, not only of the shirt industry of Derry, but of the whole of the British textile economy. For a time the

Derry factories sent work out to Morocco, until even that succumbed to the practices of the Far East. As for the outworkers, there was no other paid work for them in the wilds of Donegal.

Arthur was a clever, liberal and cultivated man who was uncomfortable in his retirement and probably saw me as a breath of fresh air from outside Northern Ireland and its petty politics. One evening he showed me a letter which had been sent to his grandmother in 1872 from Dresden by Agnes, daughter of William Tillie, a student at the finishing school run by **The Geddes Sisters, Jane, Margaret and Charlotte,** assisted by the Gräfin (Countess) Maczyneta.

Although Saxony had just been absorbed into the German Empire, Dresden was still the city of Wagner and Weber and retained all the trappings of one of the richest capitals of Europe.

> Dresdeners of all classes thought they lived in one of the most beautiful, cultured and well-administered cities in… Europe… in a … seemingly unchanged backdrop of time-honoured beauty combined with judicious modernity.

This they were happy to share with foreign residents and tourists – and there were 4,000 or more British and American residents.

John Geddes was a farmer's son in the parish of Glass, near Huntly, in Aberdeenshire (Gordon country). Glass was blessed with an excellent village dominie. John had aspirations and became a bookseller in Huntly, However, his father died and he returned to farming. He was able to push his children forward, however. He made a success of that, without having his own ambitions satisfied. His oldest son became Professor Sir William Geddes, Principal of Aberdeen University. Another son became a judge in Bengal, where he died. Alexander went to the United States, where he established himself as 'the Corn King' before returning to London where he set himself up as a gentleman in the West End. (Two of his sons were killed in World War I. Captain John Geddes of the 16th Canadian Infantry and 7/9 Cameron Highlanders was killed in 1915 in the recapture of four 4.7 guns temporarily abandoned in an action north of Ypres. John had married into the Tillie family, a daughter of Marshall Tillie, a twin son of William Tillie.)

The Geddes sisters were 'all given a really good education' by Arthur Stephen of the parish school. Within a few years they had 'been enabled to amass a fortune from their educational establishment at Dresden' and when Charlotte and Jane retired they:

> … left the seminary in such a condition that their successors may soon realize a comfortable competence for life.

Agnes Tillie's letter gives a good picture of the regime at the school, which was an interesting amalgam of academic study, aesthetic and social experiences.

Anna Morton (1857-1917) spent the year of 1875 in Dresden, studying music and equipping herself to earn her own living as a teacher of music. Although she probably did not attend the Misses Geddes's establishment she could hardly be unaware of it and of the quality of the girls who attended it.

Anna's father was Frazer Morton, an Ulster Scot who was a prosperous linen merchant in Liverpool and a strict Presbyterian, yet prepared to let his daughter disappear for a year to a foreign country. On return, Anna set up her own girls' club, near the family home, networked with Octavia Hill and others of that ilk and was involved in the incipient movement for the emancipation of women.

Her younger sister, Edith, had married James Oliphant, headmaster of the Charlotte Square (Edinburgh) Institution for the Education of Girls. The Oliphants in their own home held 'Secular Positivist' meetings on social problems. On a visit from Liverpool Anna was introduced to Patrick Geddes and must, at once, have associated the Geddes name with her happy year in Dresden with steady and reliable girls and where she began to break away from the church of her parents.

Anna Morton and Patrick Geddes were well-matched. They had the same moral compass. They were both moved by 'the new spirit of social service' and 'both had a streak of puritan severity in their idealism'. Anna, the blue stocking, in marrying Patrick Geddes, was able to share many of his ideals but managed to keep the family together and to moderate some of her dynamic husband's enthusiasms. For example, Geddes wrote brilliantly and often on the importance of Home Education, but it was Anna who managed the education of their three children – pretty successfully!

As I implied at the start, this is not a simple topic. The issues are complex and the relationships between the various players are complicated, as are their loyalties. But now it is back to July, 1893 and the Countess of Aberdeen in the Donegal Highlands and Derry My sources are the Derry/Londonderry newspapers, both generous in their coverage.

In the summer of 1893 the Aberdeens had no Governmental status in Ireland and were about to set off to the Governor-Generalship of Canada. It was therefore as a private person, although one with the authority of membership of charitable organisations, that Ishbel stepped off the train at Sligo to commence her tour. There is no mention of great formality or a great column of followers, but she had a private secretary, Miss O'Brien and a 'modest suite'. She was met at the station and escorted throughout by Mr W L Micks, secretary to the Congested Districts Board (set up by Balfour two years previously) who had made all the arrangements for the trip.

In a reflection on the state of the roads the first stage of the expedition was by the Sligo and Glasgow Steam Packet Company's boat across Donegal Bay, making a special stop at Teelin Harbour for Carrick where the villagers pulled out all the stops to welcome their distinguished visitor.

> The village was illuminated in honour of the Countess's visit, and bonfires were lighted on the adjoining hills. The village band turned out and serenaded her ladyship. Torches and bonfires were borne in the crowd, and the crowd continued to cheer until a late hour.

All this happened on a Sunday – which would not have gone down well in Scotland in the 'nineties! On Monday the party set off at 0900 for Ardara (1230), Glenties (1400) and Donegal town (1900) where they were received with a salute of small cannon, and several flags were hung out of the trees and on flagstaffs.

This must have been a busy day and resulted in four reports in the *Journal and Sentinel,* two of them identical. The fullest was in *The Derry Journal* of July 19th, 1893, under the headings *Lady Aberdeen's Tour: Journey Through Donegal.*

First stop was 'the house of the Gaffagans, where the manufacture of home-spun tweed is carried on'. We are told how important this cottage industry was in the highlands of Donegal. Lady Aberdeen spoke highly of the quality and durability of the home-spun products and wanted to compare 'the method of the Donegal peasantry with that of the Kerry weavers'. She spent time examining the weaving machines set up in the Gaffagans house and operated by the three sons.

The wool was spun in the house or in the cottages of the neighbours, to be woven into tweeds. Natural undyed wool gave 'a beautiful effect of grey' by the blending of threads from black and white sheep. Local herbs and 'bog stuff' were also used to give fast colours.

The party then moved on to Ardara where Rev Father O'Doherty presented an address to which the Countess 'briefly replied'. Lady Aberdeen visited several shops in the town where they sold local products – tweeds, knittings, laces and sprigging work. Sprigging work was once common in Ireland, but was dying out.

> It is a species of embroidery on linens, muslins etc, the figures being raised on the surface of the cloth, and is not unlike Mountmellick work, except that the figures are in relief on both sides….The linen or lawn is sent from Belfast to shopkeepers (in Ardara), who act in the capacity of middlemen, and parcel out the work among the peasant girls of the district. Some of the work was very beautiful and Lady Aberdeen was enthusiastic in speaking of its artistic excellence…and warmly suggested that monthly prizes should be offered for the best pieces of work brought in.

Surprise was felt in the hosiery department when it was discovered that nearly all the yarn used in the making of stockings was English or Scottish spun.

> A couple of tons of yarn were seen in one establishment, and not a hank of it was Irish.

Two suggestions were made, that a spinning mill be established to service the institutes among the peasantry, and that tuition be given in these districts for the dyeing of wool.

Glenties was reached at two o'clock. After luncheon at the hotel the Countess visited the different establishments in which the work of the cottagers was offered for sale. She examined with great interest samples of the stockings, gloves etc submitted to her, and expressed the pleasure she felt at seeing the evidence of an industry so well established in the mountains of Donegal.

Said *The Derry Journal:*

> It speaks well for a lady of such high rank to show her sympathy with the people, and by efforts such as these the desire she has to benefit them. During the time her husband was Lord Lieutenant she encouraged in every way the wearing of Irish manufactured goods... and will be sure not to forget the interests of Ireland wherever she can further them.

Advantage was taken of the presence of the man from the Congested Districts Board to point out that something needed to be done about the finishing of the cloth and the shrinking and milling.

Halfway to Donegal the party were received with a salute of small cannon, and several flags were hung out on the trees and on flagstaffs. Dr John O'Donnell, brother of the Bishop of Raphoe, welcomed Lady Aberdeen to the district. Donegal was reached about seven o'clock. Lady Aberdeen was the guest of Major and Mrs Hamilton at Brownhill, Ballindra.

In my wardrobe are two fine Donegal Tweed jackets with the label 'Magee'. The Central Business District of Donegal Town is a triangular square, on one side of which is Magee's, a large store, with a café and restaurant and workshops behind. As well as merely selling clothes, Magee's makes clothing from cloth woven by hand in about 200 homes in the county. The tradition lives on! And successfully! It is ironic that here, in Donegal Town, some of the old ways still bumble along, successfully filling a niche market, while, in progressive Londonderry the great factories have been demolished or recycled as flats or supermarkets.

On Tuesday morning her ladyship drove to Donegal Railway Station, arriving in Strabane shortly before half-past one. On the way she would have passed through Stranorler.

One of the delights - and hazards - of newspaper research is the proximity of other stories, sometimes more intriguing than one's subject. Beside Lady Aberdeen's movements all week was 'the alleged shooting case in Stranorler'. At the Court of Petty Sessions in Stranorler on Wednesday 19 July two men came up for hearing on an alleged shooting. After much wrangling over expenses, the magistrates adjourned the case for a week and the two accused were released on bail.

The *Londonderry Sentinel* detected a sectarian element in the case and fulminated against 'other Nationalist papers' as follows:

> The whole account turns out to have been a tissue of lies… just as the Derry Journal's story of the Stranorlar shooting outrage was a malicious fabrication. A complete refutation is published not from the pen of an Orange partisan but of a priest... He sweeps away the whole lying story in a single sentence which is as follows – "There were no party cries, there was no riot, no stones were thrown, no Orange party was driven back, no Orange flag was being seized, no persons were injured, no police were badly or at all beaten in the scuffle, there was no scuffle, and there will be no prosecutions, extensive or otherwise." The Irish News is compelled to eat humble pie under this tremendous exposure. It is likely that for some time to come Stranorler…will not be so much as named by Nationalist writers.

Much as I would have liked to follow the case through to its conclusion duty compelled me to focus on Strabane and Ishbel's reception there. She proceeded from the station to the Town Hall:

> ...which was well filled, the audience comprising a number of those

interested in the industries of the district.

Mrs Hamilton (not the hostess of the previous evening) took the chair and somewhat equivocally welcomed Lady Aberdeen. She had had Lady Aberdeen's own word that she wished to work on non-political lines and wished to meet her with every kindly feeling although 'she and I are as far apart...as we can be.'

Lady Aberdeen spoke at great length about the Irish Industries Association and the Irish Village in Chicago. Mr E Brown got two lines on the necessity for the Irish introducing better breeds of poultry. In seconding the vote of thanks Miss Sinclair (note all the Scottish names!) grumpily said the IAI could do less for the Strabane district than for Donegal.

Lady Aberdeen was afterwards conducted through the Convent, and subsequently visited the branch factory of Messrs Stapley and Smith. Her ladyship arrived in Londonderry at six o'clock (being met at the Great Northern terminus by Mr William Tillie DL and Mrs Reid) and drove in Mr Tillie's carriage to Duncreggan.

Another constant feature running alongside Lady Aberdeen in the Press was 'The Collection of County Cess in Gweedore'. Gweedore was a hotbed of nationalism. Parnell had advised tenants to offer what they considered a fair rent and, if their offer was refused, to pay no rent at all. In the parishes of Raymunterdoney and Tullaghobegley the uncollected County Cess (local tax) amounted to £1,609 and £1,989, respectively. Daniel Boyle, a tax collector, had left the country, owing the county £563. The Donegal Grand Jury was attempting to clear up the mess, but was finding it difficult to recruit district collectors.

On Thursday (20th July) the *Sentinel* commented on Lady Aberdeen's visit to Strabane. Her reception had been enthusiastic, all sensible people fully recognising the non-sectarian and non-political character of her mission and the thoroughly philanthropic aim of a movement to which she had given so great a stimulus. In a swipe at the Nationalists who enthusiastically cheered her ladyship's claim to political neutrality, readers were reminded that, when Balfour came to Donegal making the same claim and with the same objects – viz, the improvement of the congested and distressed districts – he was 'groaned at'.

> But it is hopeless to expect Nationalists to show fair play. They will recognise political neutrality if claimed by a Gladstonian, but they will not tolerate it on the part of a Unionist. Of course, Lady Aberdeen cannot be held responsible for this, but it is an aspect of the situation that she might well reflect on.

Readers were reminded also that Lady Aberdeen had seen and borne testimony to the industry and comparative prosperity of the North. That industry and prosperity had been attained under the same laws as prevailed in other parts of the country where the local natural conditions were even more favourable, and yet where she said there was a lamentable lack of enterprise and industry.

The writer sounded a warning note.

> Will the men who have created industries in Derry and the North transfer their capital, their enterprise and their industry to the backward regions which Lady Aberdeen wishes to develop? They will certainly not do so; and more than that, it is quite possible that, under the new order of things they would leave Ireland altogether. It is well known that several of the biggest shirt-making firms have been instituting enquiries in the North of England as to the possibility of transferring their factories there in the event of Home Rule being carried.

Wednesday was a busy day for Ishbel, who wore a green poplin dress and paid a further compliment to Irish sentiment by having diamond earrings of shamrock pattern. Had she looked at the local papers at breakfast she would have noted:

MAIL NEWS – ALLAN LINE

The Royal Mail steamer Parisian, of this celebrated line, which sailed from Moville for Quebec on the evening of the 14th inst., arrived out yesterday – all well – making the run in less than a week. The succeeding steamers of this line are the steamship Namibian, sailing to Quebec on the 28th inst. carrying her Majesty's mails; the steamship Scandinavian direct to Boston on the 27th Inst. and that magnificent steamer the State of California direct to New York on Saturday, the 29th inst.. Passengers will please note. The steamship Prussian arrived at Boston on 20th inst. - all well.

And in the *Londonderry Sentinel:*

LONDONDERRY SHIP NEWS
ARRIVED

Confidence ss Cardiff, coal
Anglesey, Bangor, slates
Cironesia ss, New York, passengers, Anchor Line
Iolanthe (yacht) Belfast, light
Tagus ss Sulina, maize
At Panama, on 17th inst, the barque Alexander Black, of Londonderry – all well

CLEARED OUT

Ivy Holmes ss, Maryport, light
Triton ss, the Baltic, ballast
Allies, Maryport, ballast
Blanche ss, Workington, light
Iolanthe, light
Nevis, Portrush, light
Florrie, Ayr, timber
Anglesey, Bangor, light
Circassia ss, Glasgow, passengers

She would have achieved very quickly an impression of the strengths and weaknesses of the North West economy as well as being quite amazed at the region's lively links with mainland Britain, Europe and the New World.

In the forenoon Lady Aberdeen 'visited and inspected with much interest and evident pleasure two of the largest of our local shirt and underclothing factories'. At Messrs Tillie and Henderson's 'extensive establishment' she 'obtained a rapid view of the different departments, including the finely-equipped laundry'.

She moved on to Messrs Welch, Margetson's premises of 1872 - 'pronounced by experts to be the most perfect factory in Ireland' – and was shown over the building. She was 'much pleased' with all she saw.

During the day she visited the principal points of interest in and around the city.

From four to seven Mr and Mrs Tillie held a reception at their house, Duncreggan, to give the leading citizens an opportunity to meet Lady Aberdeen. This was in the form of a garden party in 'the beautifully situated and prettily-kept grounds and gardens', with refreshments dispensed in the dining room. A large marquee was erected on the lawn and in it Lady Aberdeen gave an address in furtherance of her scheme of industrial development.

The guest list numbered over 700. There were the usual civic heads, the Bishop, Dean and Reverend Canon of Derry (Church of Ireland), quite a string of ministers – but no Catholic priests. There were three professors and quite a handful of doctors. A majority of the names were clearly of English or Lowland Scottish origin – Beresford, Babington, Miller, Allen and, of course, Hogg. (Mr and Mrs D Hogg were present. This may have been David Cleghorn Hogg, who was a leading citizen, even if he was a Home Ruler). But there was also a fair sprinkling of names which could have been native Irish or Scots Gaelic, like, for example, Campbell. Thus there were the Misses M'Connell and District Inspector O'Connell, Conolly and Milligan.

And what are we to make of Mr Conolly Gage?

Mr Tillie, who chaired the occasion, was fulsome in his praise of Lady Aberdeen, saying that there could be:

> ...but one feeling as to the spirit of self-sacrifice and earnest determination which animated her ladyship and he trusted that success would crown her efforts, and that her mission would be as encouraging and as successful as she wished.

Visiting speakers always try to win over their audience with some local references and a joke. Lady Aberdeen started by rehearsing the virtues of Londonderry and its entrepreneurs, which went down well. As did the joke. She moved on to her Irish Industries Association and its work. Derry was the home of home industries and the two should complement and support each other.

The Dean of Derry in proposing the vote of thanks struck a slightly patronising note in comparing his city with other districts that were 'less favourably circumstanced'. He had great pleasure in handing Lady Aberdeen £5 for her excellent work. (To the 21st century reader £5 might appear a calculated insult, but £5 in 1893 would be equivalent to £500 today).

In the evening Ishbel had second thoughts about the meeting and from Duncreggan wrote to the Editor of the Sentinel. Regrets had been expressed to her after the meeting that she had not mentioned more definitely the arrangements for receiving the names of those desirous of becoming members or subscribers. She now added a little note of what had to be done. She mentioned also that the Dean of Derry and Mrs Smyly, Mr Tillie and Mr Cooke had each been good enough to place £5 on the subscription list.

She went on to say how she had appreciated the kindness she had received and had felt encouraged in her work of developing the home industries of Ireland. She finished by offering the services of the Association to the ladies of Derry.

A letter appeared in the *Derry Journal* on Monday morning 31st July from the Bishop's House, Derry. The RC Bishop apologized for not having been able to meet Lady Aberdeen when she was in Derry, but he was then engaged in the annual retreat of the clergy, from which he could not conveniently excuse himself.

He wrote that Lady Aberdeen had set a noble example and was glad to see that many Irish ladies were lending her valuable assistance. He hoped that more would join her movement and 'bring to many a poor family the comforts to which they have been strangers so long'.

He enclosed £5 for the fund and was 'sorry that the constant calls upon me prevent my being able to send you more'.

The Countess of Aberdeen left Derry for Dublin by the first train on the Great Northern Railway on the Thursday morning. At Monaghan she received an address and at Drogheda she was presented with a number of addresses. In replying, her last words on the trip summed up its success very well.

Home industries are carried on there and all around to perfection. They went there perhaps, with an ulterior object, inasmuch as they hoped some day the large houses in Derry would help the association by taking over some of the workers whom they hoped to train in the earlier stages of work in the West of Ireland. They had hopes that if they were able to train some of those workers who need work so badly at Derry that by-and-bye houses in association with the trade would take on those workers. She had been received so kindly at Derry that she hoped such might be the case. However, Derry was willing to help them, for a promise had been made that a sale for Irish goods would be organized and held in that city next year.

Lady Aberdeen had had a busy week. The following week was to be spent in Scotland – her reason for being unable to attend the Strabane Games. Her authority on the visit was a touch equivocal. Her husband sat in the House of Lords, but he was 'between jobs' and she no longer had the authority of a Vicereine. But the visit was stage-managed and organised and she was accompanied throughout by a government official. She stayed as a guest in private houses. As the Chairman (!) of the Irish Industries Association she could not dictate or decree, but had to flatter and cajole.

In Donegal she was feted and flattered as she made her visits of inspection. There was no sign of oppressive landlords or gombeenmen, but, as an intelligent woman, she must have been able to work out to what extent her experience was representative. She must also have noted the importance of the Catholic priesthood in the community.

In Strabane and Derry she was welcomed and praised for her efforts in improving the lot of 'the Donegal cottagers'. But it was also made plain that the Derry entrepreneurs were doing very nicely, thank you, and did not really see the necessity to change their ways. It was an 'us and them' situation – but they were prepared to help 'them' - but only in so far as it suited their objectives. If we look at the last sentence of the *Sentinel* report above, that seems to be a pretty poor return for her week's work.

The split in Irish society between Nationalist/Catholics and Protestant/Unionists is clear from the reporting of the two local newspapers. Although many items in both papers were identical, written by the same hand, there were differences, usually reflecting the political stances of the two papers.

This is summarized very neatly when Ishbel died and her death was reported in the North West.

The *Derry Journal* of 19th April 1939 was quite terse.

Ishbel, Dowager Marchioness of Aberdeen and Temair, died at her home, Gordon House, Rubislaw Den, North Aberdeen, yesterday, aged 82. Her death was due to heart failure. Her husband, the first Marquis, died five years ago.

Now, from the *Londonderry Sentinel* of 20th April 1939:

Ishbel, Dowager Marchioness of Aberdeen and Temair, died at her home, Gordon House, Rubislaw Den, North Aberdeen, on Tuesday. She had not been well for some time.
Lady Aberdeen was the wife of the first Marquis.
In Ireland Lady Aberdeen was esteemed for her sympathetic understanding of social problems. On two occasions – in 1886 and again from 1905 to 1915 – Lord Aberdeen was Lord Lieutenant of Ireland. While in this country Lady Aberdeen inaugurated an anti-tuberculosis campaign, and it was she who founded the Women's National Health Association of Ireland. She was also prominently associated with the Irish Industries Association.

The following appeared in the *Derry Journal* of 3rd May:

DONEGAL HOMESPUN WORKERS REGRETS
Tributes were paid to the late Lady Aberdeen and regret expressed at her death at a meeting of Donegal homespun workers at Ardara on Saturday, Mr C Gallagher presiding.
Regret was also expressed at the death of Rev P Confery, (?) Clona, one of the pioneers of the homespun.

On 4th May the same notice appeared in the Sentinel under the headline - TRIBUTE TO LADY ABERDEEN.

It may appear strange that the community that benefitted least from Lady Aberdeen's efforts should give her more credit than the other, but this is not really surprising. Revolutionaries find it very difficult to recognise any good in those from whom they extracted power. At the centenary celebrations in 2012 of the Peamount Sanatorium in Dublin, for which Lady Aberdeen was the leading driving force, there was no mention of her. Tucked into a back street near a canal in Cork is a miserable little memorial to those killed in the First World War. The last time I saw it, it had had white paint thrown over it. Trivial but annoying. The Nelson Pillar in O'Connell Street in Dublin was severely damaged by explosives planted by Irish republicans and the remnants destroyed.

Finally, in Londonderry, opposite the site of Tillie's factory, the 'Hands across the Divide' statue of 1992 by Maurice Harron (PLATE 4b)) is a simple expression of hope. It used to be respected but has recently had white paint splashed across it. Rosita Borland in the Irish Times is cheaply cynical about it.

> Finally, the twee Hands Across the Divide statues in Derry by Maurice Harron is another aberration that never fails to make me grit my teeth when I see it. It's two men, reaching out hands to each other. Across a divide. It's clumsy and pointless and about as sophisticated a public statement on politics as Gerry Adam's tweets of his teddy bears are.

How important can a short week in the North West have been in a life of 82 years? Her visit must have reassured Ishbel of the worth of her activities in advancing and promoting the cause of Irish domestic manufactures, so that she was able to move on to Canada and the United States and proselytise with confidence. But she must also have realized that, however successful this movement might have been, it was not going to bring about any fundamental change in the situation. Ireland needed more fundamental change.

Thus it was that, when the Gordons came back to Dublin for the second time, Lady Gordon turned her attention to public health and disease prevention, and to environmental improvement through careful planning.

The tragedy was that the new Irish Free State threw the baby out with the bath water and rejected her innovations as Imperialist meddling. 'The jagged edge between soft-focus de Valeran rhetoric and the hard reality of emigration, stagnation and deprivation was carefully erased' in the search for 'a whole and useful Christian life'. Ishbel's proposals and achievements were allowed to run into the sand or were taken over and claimed by others.

Appendix 1

Functions of Central Organisation of WNHAI

1. Sutton Preventorium and Holiday Home
2. The PF Collier Memorial Dispensary
9. Samaritan Committee's Work*
4. Allan A Ryan Home Hospital for Consumption
5. Farm for Cases where Disease is Arrested
6. After-care of Patients
7. Pasteurised Milk Depot
8. Deficient Milk Supply and the Vice-Regal Milk Commission
9. Infant Mortality Work*
10. Health Lecturers
11. Lantern Health Lectures
12. Children Suffering from Tuberculosis
13. Formation of Irish Goat Society and Improvement of Irish Goats
14. Heating and Cleaning of National Schools
15. Night Camp for Working Boys in Dublin
16. Publication of Health Literature
17. Travelling Health Exhibition
18. Blue Bird Health Travelling Caravan
19. Transformation of Derelict Town Spaces into Garden Playgrounds
20. Formation of Housing and Town Planning Association of Ireland
21. Health and Industries Exhibition
22. Co-operation of Central Association with Health Authorities
23. The Association's Work under the National Insurance Act of 1911
24. Scheme to Supplement the Salaries of Duly Qualified Midwives in Outlying Districts in Ireland in order that Skilled Attendance may be available for mothers in those districts
American Sister Branches
Finance

* This is the order and labelling printed in the Report.

Appendix 2

PATRICK GEDDES

Patrick Geddes had an excellent working relationship with the Aberdeens and supported their endeavours. Plate 2a suggests how complicated his life must have been. This is supported by his entry in Who's Who of 1930, which is given below.
Almost certainly, this was written by Geddes himself and should be read with that fact in mind.
That there is no mention of Ireland or Dublin suggests that he did not see his Irish involvement as a success or even worthy of note.

Extract from Who's Who – 1930

GEDDES, Patrick, late Professor of Sociology and Civics, University of Bombay; Professor of Botany (retired), Univ. College, Dundee (St. Andrews Univ.); Senior Resident of Univ. Hall, Edinburgh; Director of the Cities and Town Planning Exhibition; b. 1854; y.s. of late Capt. Alex. Geddes; m. 1st, 1886, Anna (d. 1917), e.d. of Frazer Morton, merchant, Liverpool; two s.one d.; 2nd, 1928, Lilian, 2nd d. of late John Armour Brown, Moredun, Paisley. Educ.: Perth Academy, Royal School of Mines, University Coll., London; Sorbonne: Univs. Of Edinburgh, Montpellier etc.. Successively Demonstrator of Physiology at Univ. Coll., London; of Zoology at Univ. at Aberdeen; of Botany at Edinburgh; Lecturer on Natural History in School of Medicine, Edinburgh; with intervals of travel, e.g. exploration in Mexico, visits to Continental universities, zoological stations, and botanic gardens, as also to Cyprus and the East, to U.S.A. etc. Studies: geography, biology, history, art, social economy and civics. Educational work (besides teaching) mainly in organisation of University Halls, Edinburgh and Chelsea, each as a beginning of collegiate life, e.g. at Edinburgh, with its Summer

Meeting and Outlook Tower. This is a regional, geographic, and synthetic type-museum, with associated undertakings of geotechnic and social purpose e.g. city improvement (Old Edinburgh, etc.), gardens, parks etc. Publishing house (Geddes and Colleagues) associated with Celtic and general literature and art, with geography, education and synthetics. Actively occupied in city improvement, town-planning, and educational initiatives at home, on continent and in India, etc. and with University designs (India, Jerusalem, etc), and development of Cite Universitaire Mediterraneanne at Montpellier. Publications: Evolution of Sex, Evolution, Sex, Biology and Life in Evolution (jointly with Prof. J. Arthur Thomson); Chapters in Modern Botany; City Development; Cities in Evolution; The Life and Work of Sir Jagadis C. Bose, F.R.S., 1920; The Coming Polity (with V.V. Branford); Ideas at War (with Prof. Gilbert Slater); Our Social Inheritance (with V.V. Branford), etc. Recreations: gardening, rambling. Address: Outlook Tower, Univ. Hall, Edinburgh; c/o Sociological Society, Leplay House, 65 Belgrave Road, S.W.1; Collège des Ecossais, Montpellier, France.

Further Reading

FHA Aalan, Kevin Whelan and Matthew Stout (eds.), Atlas of the Irish Rural Landscape (Cork University Press, Cork, 1997)

Jonathan Bardon, The Plantation of Ulster (Gill and Macmillan, Dublin, 2011)

Walter Stephen (ed.), Learning from the Lasses: Women of the Patrick Geddes Circle (Luath Press, Edinburgh, 2014)

Frank Sweeney, The Letterkenny and Burtonport Extension Railway 1903-47: Its Social context and Environment goes Unpublished PhD Thesis, National University of Ireland, Maynooth, 2004)

Some other books by Walter Stephen

The Gypsy Empresses: A Study in Escapism

In the 1890s there were a number of Empresses around in Europe. Some were quite accepting of the double standard, happy to put up with convention for the sake of the jewels, the dresses and the adoration of the public. Others were not. The Empress Elisabeth of Austria went walkabout. Carlota (of Mexico) was driven mad by her errant husband and his crazy ambitions. Even our own Queen Victoria, Empress of India, had her mild rebellions.

THE GYPSY EMPRESSES
A STUDY IN ESCAPISM

The top favourite refuge was the Mediterranean coast, the Riviera, the Cote d'Azur, where winters were mild, 'where the lemon trees bloom', where every pleasure was catered for and where congenial company was to be found.

In **The Gypsy Empresses** Walter Stephen tells us what brought these great ladies from Russia, France, Germany, Austria, and Britain to the Riviera and what happened when the Empires crashed and two world wars disturbed the social order.

The Gypsy Empresses (ISBN 978-0-9555190-3-1, 190 pp, 19 colour plates, 10 B/W illustrations) is published by Hills of Home at the UK price of £12.99.

Copies are available directly from the author at the special price of £8 (p&p included). Cheques should be made payable to;
Walter M Stephen
Hills of Home
82 Pentland Terrace
EDINBURGH
EH10 6HF

The Evolution of Evolution: Darwin, Enlightenment and Scotland

In 1825, at the age of 16, Darwin began to study medicine at the University of Edinburgh, the seat of the Enlightenment. The Enlightenment had created a thirst for science, and in his two years at Edinburgh, Darwin became involved with the people and ideas that were to shape the world's understanding of the natural sciences. These people and theories had immense influence on the evolution of Darwin's concept of natural selection.

An earlier book, *Vestiges of the Natural History of Creation* by Scotsman Robert Chambers, led the way for *On the Origin of Species,* and influenced Darwin's writing and studies. Fellow Scot James Hutton, 'the founder of modern geology', established that the earth was far older than the previously estimated 6,000 years, and Charles Lyell, born in Scotland, developed this theory into a book that Darwin took with him on the *Beagle,* and to which he owed many of his later discoveries.

Walter Stephen considers the impact these men, and many others, had on Darwin's work, his writings, and his life. He looks at the changing views of Darwin in his own lifetime, and at the legacy he left to science and to the world.

Well researched and thoughtfully written. SCOTTISH REVIEW OF BOOKS

The Evolution of Evolution
(ISBN 1-906817-23-5 164 pp, 18 B/W illustrations)
is published by Luath Press at the
UK price of £12.99.

Copies are available directly from the author
at the special price of £8 (p&p included).
Cheques should be made payable to;
Walter M Stephen
Hills of Home
82 Pentland Terrace
EDINBURGH

A Dirty Swindle: True Stories of Scots in the Great War

Walter Stephen provides an uninhibited look at the misery and toil of World War I through a collection of twelve stories. Providing a Scottish perspective, he takes a look at reports from home and abroad with scepticism, delving deeper to unveil the unencumbered truth.

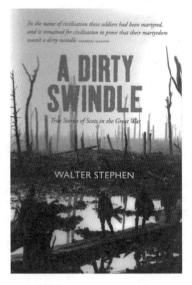

Recalling Siegfried Sassoon's words, Stephen reveals how the failures of those in command in the Great War became known as A Dirty Swindle. The varied accounts chronicle the progress of troops from recruitment to training to the front line, as well as revealing a side of Field Marshal Haig never seen before and which will be a revelation to historians.

He is sceptical about some of the myths being perpetrated in the name of commemoration. He does not wallow in sentiment - only two deaths are described in detail - but, above all, he staggers us with the sheer immensity, complexity - and misery - of the Great Struggle.

Yet all is not unrelievedly dark. Some of the stories reveal the courage and selflessness of both combatants and non-combatants and a few dying communities were saved by the changed priorities of wartime.

It seems harder than ever to hear something new about the First World War, but Stephen gave us that. THE HERALD

A Dirty Swindle is published by Luath Press in hardback and paperback. Hardback ISBN is 978-1-910745-13-7 with 190 pp, 17 plates and 13 B/W illustrations at a UK price of £126.99. The paperback ISBN is 978-1-910745-99-1. It has the same content as the hardback at the UK price of £9.99.

Copies are available directly from the author at the special price of £10 (Hardback) or £8 (Paperback) (p&p included).
Cheques should be made payable to;
Walter M Stephen
Hills of Home
82 Pentland Terrace
EDINBURGH
EH10 6HF